Fire and Ice

An Anthology of Collaborations

Creative Talents Unleashed

Anthologies Published by Creative Talents Unleashed

Microaggression ~ Then & Now

Cupid's Arrow

I Have a Name

Down The Rabbit Hole

Poetic Shadows – Ink and the Sword

Imperfect Paths

Shades of the Same Skin

Poetic Melodies

Divided Lines – A Poet's Stance

Writing Tips – Exploring the Writer's Path

Unleashed

Love, a Four Letter Word

All Proceeds from our anthologies are donated to the Starving Artist Fund which helps publish authors at no cost. For more info please visit

www.ctupublishinggroup.com/starving-artist-fund.html

GENERAL INFORMATION

Fire and Ice

By

Creative Talents Unleashed

1st Edition: 2018

This Publishing is protected under Copyright Law as a "Collection". All rights for all submissions are retained by the Individual Author and or Artist. No part of this publishing may be Reproduced, Transferred in any manner without the prior **WRITTEN CONSENT** of the "Material Owner" or its Representative Creative Talents Unleashed.

Creative Talents Unleashed

www.ctupublishinggroup.com

Publisher Information
1st Edition: Creative Talents Unleashed
info@ctupublishinggroup.com

This Collection is protected under U.S. and International Copyright laws

Copyright © 2018: Creative Talents Unleashed

ISBN-13: 978-1-945791-57-4 (Creative Talents Unleashed)

Credits

Book Cover
Raja Williams

Creative Director
Sarah Lamar King

Editor
All Writer's Responsible For Own Work

Foreword
Lyne Beringer

Foreword

Many moons ago I realized the power of words and how they can accurately describe the nuances of emotion. They can take a person to the highest highs, and just as easily, that person can plummet into nothingness.... just by words. It is fascinating how perception and illusion rule our lives. What others fail to see is that for some, once the words are out there... the bleeding stops a little bit more... Those words are just part of us...And that is the beauty of it.

Fire and Ice is a collection of connections based on perceptions. It is person after person, reading, relating, and then reaching out to others through words. Connection... is really what it is all about that.

I am honored to invite you inside the minds of people just like you. All their hopes, dreams, and disasters are here within the pages of this book.

Lyne Beringer, author of *Alaskan Vogue*

"Write something so inspirational it sets people's minds and pens on fire."

-Sarah Lamar King

Table of Contents

Foreword	v
Fire and Ice	1
All That Glitters	4
Corner of Paradise & Madness St.	5
Distant	6
Mask	7
Man on the Moon	9
Protest Songs	10
Survive	12
Appointment at Sarajevo	13
The Imposter	14
Lopsided Within My Lean	15
Burned	19
The Price of Sweet Revenge	20
After Midnight	21
Winter Falls	23
Wings	27
Tuesday's Gone	28
Comradery	32
Chain	33
Here	37
Poverty it was You ~ The cry of the poor	38
Fire of the Phoenix	40
Hope	41
Doubt	42
Concrete Jungle	44
Broken Lands	46
Unspoken	48
Our Time	51
A Beginner's Fortune	54
Steps	55
Day of Remembrance	56

Reality's Sorrow	57
Meant To Be	58
Crevices of Pain	59
Writers Block	61
Memories	65
Infernos	66
Traveler	67
Interred Truth	68
When I Die	69
Job of Living	71
My Enemy/My Friend	72
Smoked	73
Fly	76
Ice to the Fire	77
Fevered Twilight, Lost and Fading	79
Night's Battle	81
Fight	82
Frigid	85
Freedom	87
Can't Escape	88
Broken Approbation	90
Walk With Me	91
Moments	93

"I never realized
How manic our love was,
But love is an odd affliction
The Cure not as satisfying
As the disease."

WjWeigand

Fire and Ice

Fire and Ice
Both of them burn
The cold and the heat
Each enjoying a turn
Fire and Ice
Instigators of change
They devour the weak
In the wars that they wage
Fire and Ice
Stealing all of my dreams
Neither are never
Quite what they seem
Fire and Ice
The gypsy in free
Delusions of grandeur
The alter ego of me

Burning in my veins
Changing my vision
Nothing will be the same
Fire and ice
Churning in my eyes
Freedom has come
From icy flames

Verse of day
Rhyme of night
One casts dawn
On another's twilight
Fire and Ice
Black and White
A tale inspired
In union to write

An Anthology of Collaborations

*Burning and cold
fighting inside.
Flames rising up
consuming the hate
ice cooling down
which one is bait?
Hot and cold
emotions so bold,
fire and ice
which one will hold?*

Cold as winter
but hot as hell
Balanced by a scale
through my mind
Cross me...
You're surely get burned
And frost bitten
by my words
Taste the sensation
of what's been fed to you
Can handle the two?

*Fire and Ice
Can deaden a soul
Scorching my heart
Boring its hole*

*Fire and Ice
Not for tepid or weak
Buyer beware
if its love that you seek
Let me burn*

An Anthology of Collaborations

in the fire
Let me freeze
in the ice
Let me melt
in your flames
death by
Fire and Ice

Lyne Beringer, *Maggie Mae*, Markus Fleiscmann,
A.M. Torres, Tammy S. Thomas, *Brenda-Lee Ranta*

All That Glitters

Not all that glitters is gold.
Not all that has age is old.
Not all that is bright is wise.
Not all that blinds you affects your eyes.

Remember that you shall reap what you sow.
Good plans by evil means never grow.

Not all that is sudden is a surprise.
Not all who enforce laws are above lies.
Not all that is dark is black.
Any time you waste you can never get back.

> *Not all that matters is spoken.*
> *Not all that shatters is broken.*
> *Not all that is dark is hidden.*
> *Not all that is thought is written.*
>
> *Forget where you have been and gone.*
> *The past is not a road to walk on.*
>
> *Not all that is expected will be.*
> *Not all that are unchained are free.*
> *Not all that is shining is light.*
> *Every wrong that is avoided is right.*

John S. Les, *Matt Eayre*

An Anthology of Collaborations

Corner of Paradise and Madness St.

Smoke rings curl up passion's ceiling
Too many shots numb this feeling
Amid neon hailstorms, I'm your desire
Think twice before tasting my fire
Chaotic sanity hangs in the balance
Incoherent lust will be your penance
Can you dance with this insanity
With handcuffed acrobatic alacrity
Here in this alternative paradise
Where madness melts the ice

If rings of smoke numb passion's feeling
I'll take just enough shots to leave me reeling
Desire rules the storms that rage
It's oblivious to the wars we wage
There is no balance to insanity
One minute lost is another free
And the cuffs are for my favorite vice
I'm the Queen of Madness.... Queen of Ice

Lasting memories of abandoned hearts
Chilled blue by yesterday's forever
Seeing into the distance
Vague images of lost warmth.
Eyes turn to the evening's blue light sky.
We search the firmaments forever.
To find the simple slivers of iced cold night

Kent Rucker, *Lyne Beringer*, Sean Christopher

An Anthology of Collaborations

Distant

I don't remember us anymore.
We were an event I know was wonderful,
but I can't quite grasp why.
You turned so cold, stayed so distant, always said no.

"I remember it like it was one minute ago."

...and just like that the memories flood back and I sigh,
knowing why it was you.

*We were the sizzle on the griddle
the fireworks on the fourth of July
the last float in the parade
I was the truth
you were a charade.*

*Every second that the clock ticks
is a deep stabbing wound
a heartfelt memory that pricks
a pain that I've come to savor*

...the delectable insanity of loving you.

Tiffany Simone, *D.B. Hall*

Mask

She hides it well,
But she has a brimstone soul
behind those permafrost eyes.
And she's willing to open
the gates to her frozen tundra
for the one who can ignite
her heart's bashful embers.

*he sees right through her mask,
but never will tell a soul
of the beauty he has seen.
standing outside the walls
has always kept him true
to the hope that one day,
he'll be allowed inside.*

It's a learned behavior,
this mask of numbness she wears.
Made up perfectly everyday, so no one
can reach that soul.
Show her your flame never stops burning,
and maybe just maybe she'll wash her face for you tonight.

*She dreams in vibrant color
and guards herself
behind rigid black and white.*

*Her standards have been set
by gallant heroes of the past
who rode for glory
and fought for love.*

Her bashful eyes

*raise from familiar pages
to accept another library card
and process a few more books.*

*During his flirtatious transaction
the warmth in her voice
is belied by the chill in her eyes
as she has read it all before.*

Alfa, *Matt Eayre*, Tiffany Simone, *D.B. Hall*

Man on the Moon

His lunacy trembled
upon her hands,
as it was written down
like a sketched silhouette,
his mind then calmed
as if it was the eye of the storm.

She helped him heal
within her wandering...
Though he was ice cold,
he is her man on the moon,
and she warms his dark side,
as they swim the soundwaves of silence.

Together they watched time
evolve, and unravel; into history
Fire, and Ice they are the blackhole mystery.

Her fire burned so bright
She could not see
Until his ice cooled her
To a tropical breeze

When he hides his face
She still feels his touch
She is his sunshine
Even when he is on the dark side

Sarah Ann Waldron, *Maggie Mae*

Protest Songs

Where are all the protest songs?

Ticket stubs, blowin' in the wind,
over trampled fences, scarred pasture
An old black man sings of freedom,
to the empty fields of Yasgur's farm

Slogans sung in faded jeans
Purple haze, We Shall Overcome
Prophetic words in hashish days
Was it only hype that youth contrived,
If in the end, it was a lie?

Where are all the protest singers?

Dated songs, too old to sing,
gated hippies, too rich too care
Six string anthems, lyrical maps,
guiding us back home

Pocket watch in a business suit
love beads on a rear-view mirror
shagging wagons turned sedan
now they all work for the man
peace is a forgotten plan

Where are all the protests gone?
Sweet leaf breezes, bombers, butterflies,
overgrown children buried in the garden
Placards in mud, posters in blood,
Woodstock is dead

Daisies dried up in their hair
succumb to their survival
wrinkled hippies sit and stare
whining from their easy chairs
mutter protests; no one cares

An old black man sings of freedom
forgotten words of protest songs
Sometimes I feel like a motherless child,
lost in the empty fields of Yasgur's farm

Brenda-Lee Ranta, Hugh Dysart

Survive

There are times when these dark, weighted emotions
become too heavy a load to carry, and I begin to sink
back into that abyss from which I crawled.
Scraped hands, bruised knees, and bloody knuckles
serve as mementos of my struggle
and my willingness to fight for survival.
Yet this intangible thing virtually has the power
to bring me to my knees, begging for reprieve.
Well not this time, my old friend.
I've incinerated our binding ties,
reducing them to nothing more than ash.
Within me burns an immortal flame,
and with each labored breath I take
the fire is steadily stoked.
For I am a master of the elements,
and you are merely another to be transmuted

I'm done with living in other's shadows
It is my time to shine
and cast all doubts firmly aside
Gather up all these loose ends
and set my universe spinning
From now on, like all prime numbers
divided evenly or only by itself
I will stand tall and be the first counted.
The first in the queue, the first in command
The first woman on earth to do everything from now on ...
For the first time in my life, I will be number one.

Dena Daigle, *Mark Andrew Heathcote*

Appointment at Sarajevo

'Next June, The Arch Duke Franz Ferdinand, heir apparent, in his capacity as Inspector General of the Austrian Army will attend the summer maneuvers of the Sixth District Army to be held in Bosnia. A visit to Sarajevo will follow ending on the 28th of June...' newspaper clipping.

The youth at the cafe table stares at the black letters,
His lips move as he rereads the words,
The white and black turn scarlet in his mind,
'I shall shatter walls and windows
and the shards shall carve the future,
My ghost shall shriek down the halls of Vienna
and rock the very throne...',
He coughs, and feels the sudden pain in his lungs,
Gavrilo says to his companions,
'Next June we have a date with destiny....'

And the world will be changed for ever.

Europe erupts
Shock -troops swarm over Serbia
As Russian cross-hairs drift west

And Prussia, must lunge to the east
With saber in hand

While Belgium
Quakes, in the slaughter

Richard Milne, *William Wright Jr.*

The Imposter

It gives … temporarily
It lifts… briefly
It speaks a lie
As though it were true
It beguiles you
It transforms you
But when the lie meets the light
You are naked
Unarmed … unprepared
For the avalanche of truth
That will bury you

*Your reflection isn't a pillar of strength
It's just a pillar of salt melting in the rain .
Ask yourself what is really real
Do you believe in that fake mask?
Hiding behind impenetrable scars …
It will only carve your insides out
Make you a charlatan
At the mercy of other weaker phonies
Who wants nothing more than to break you?
Don't be self-hoaxed self-loathing
Don't be putty in their evil hands
Mirror, mirror on the wall I hate you
But I remember how you made me your pawn
And somehow, I drown in your depths
Only to survive and smash you
Mirror, mirror on the wall
I no longer heed your call
I should have broken you a long time before.*

Xavier Smith, *Mark Andrew Heathcote*

Lopsided Within My Lean

Sometimes I'm lopsided,
Unsure of which way to lean,
Is it my weight that you will carry?
As the unclear becomes seen...

Pressure explodes, turning all into pain...
Directing me to explore alternatives
Finding myself in complete anguish,
Having no choice in being more assertive

I'm climaxing within this wind
Which is full of bad vibes
And I can't ignore these feelings,
Nor can I keep on within my oblige

I'm fighting away the darkness,
Which creeps up my back to cripple
And I cannot relieve the pain,
That keep stirring up these ripples

I'm one foot out the door,
But I just can't seem to leave...
My heart is glued to yours,
And it's the love I'm trying to retrieve...

But I can't keep on feeling this way,
Like love is being sucked from me
And I just can't keep on breathing this way...
Feeling unsure of which way to lean

My insides are feeling all hollowed out
Yes, I've been tossed aside before
But this time is different it's a drought

My heart is wilting, dried up to the core.

I listen intently for any reason to stay
There are only lies on top of lies
What we had ripe fruit rots, and fades away
I take comfort in the mold that slowly dies.

How it lingers to survive, but untimely croaks!
This now how it feels holding your photograph,
The fire is dead, it no longer sparks smokes
And your old love letters read like an epitaph.

Love hearts and kisses engraved on a tomb,
I ask myself which way you lean
But plain as day there's nothing to exhume
All I need now, a match and some gasoline.

I ask myself which way I lean
Finding myself with one foot still in the door
Vying this darkness back into its ravine
I, wanting you back once more.

I made bold
My intents,
Questions came;
I whisper them
In dreams,
They call me sick;
I share them
In grief,
They mock me.
So I kept quiet
Let them into chambers

Of conceit and insolence.

Read me
If you can
Or see my lines
If they can help;
I will see beyond
You
Though I reside
Under your heel
Presently.

Broken and defeated.
You will not keep me down.
I will rise from your oppression,
from your drought.
I will seek out new pastures,
drink from the well of love, and
I will be set free.
I will abandon your desert of rejection.
Your uncaring touch, barren of emotion.
I will crawl on hands and knees, till
rain falls upon my broken body.
I will soak up my tears.
Hydrating my tissues and cells.
I will rise once more and leave you
Burning in the sands of bitterness.

My heart will flow freely from gaps unable to be plugged.
I have prayed feverishly for you
to baptize yourself in the pureness of my confessions.
But alas, you remain dry.
I am terrified at how seamless you turn emotions

An Anthology of Collaborations

On and off like a faucet.
Flowing hot one moment and cold the next.
You bathe your ego in my wanting,
leaving me dirty with regret.

Elle McLin, *Mark Andrew Heathcote*, Dagu Shangevlumun, *Amanda J. Evans*, Amy Noble

Burned

When you were undressing me, your touch burned
I felt the lace of my panties melting into my skin
Your lips tasted like Red Hots as I sweetly bit
The passion between us set afire
Should I trust a man who burns me?

When the fire of passion burns low,
Yet it may reignite tomorrow's glow.

To be burned
By another's desires
To invite whispered nothing's
Of a liar
Is carelessly playing with fire
To be burned
Scorched
Is to offer a heart once whole
To be forever changed
Into a lump of coal
Charred
Torn apart
The remnants of a fading
Spark

Kelly Klein, *Richard Milne*, Markus Fleiscmann

The Price of Sweet Revenge

The smoke plumes have withered away
But at what cost?
A sword, is returned to its sheath
But the nights still teem with the lost

War is no game I've been told,
Yet that is the way it's often sold,
Those who believe it may find a fate,
The price of winning is known too late
The world moves on its lurching way,
But many will never see that day.

War is heroic so many believe,
with death and destruction, there is no reprieve.
To kill one for something they don't understand,
hate manufactured it gets out of hand.

William Wright Jr., *Richard Milne*, A.M. Torres

After Midnight

Ink bleeds out onto the paper
The room is sticky hot
I've got a pit down in my stomach
It's tied up all in knots
Years went sliding through my fingers
Lines look deeper in my skin
Age is gaining some momentum
Turns out that death is what I win
So my pen is extrication
I write my words out loud to God
It's my one way first class ticket
After I break free of this facade
Ink bleeds on past the paper
Forming pools upon the floor
I'd bet a dollar no one's listening
Except the ghosts outside my door

That have vanquished the living sun
And want to linger all day
Whilst I bleed out my heart benumb
Penning every empty cliché
That has ever been sung by a drunk
Without the will to moderate
to get off a bar stool and debunk
All those lies they indoctrinated
Ink bleeds like a river
Ink bleeds from a fissure
Ink bleeds and I wither
Ink bleeds but I'm a caterpillar
And I'm a gonna be a butterfly just you wait and see

The night wanes, the moon rises high
my familiar friend

a fan turns and hums
a thought turns in my mind as well
for a thread dangles there
waiting for me to grasp it
in the darkness of a vacuum.

I grasp the glowing thread
and weave a vibrant web
an exciting tale
while my eyes droop
knowing tomorrow I will pay the price.

Yet at times the thread proves to be elusive
dancing beyond my outstretched thoughts
fading away into the darkness
or blending into a rave of multi-colored threads
a sea of disjointed thoughts.

Sleep captures me
only so I can be awakened later
by the pricking of an excited muse
bleeding my thoughts
I dip my pen quickly in
and write away my sleep.

My Muse is a weaver
that knows no time nor place
a puppet master in the darkness
a spirit walker
a ghost in my dreams
it is all a fantasy
yet it is my reality.

Lyne Beringer, *Mark Andrew Heathcote*, D.B. Hall

Winter Falls

The love is gone
Why are we still running
in circles here?
The feelings that were once true
has disappeared
Empty halls and shallow walls of a house that was a home
Is now filled with cold air
No one's feelings we have to spare
Our hearts are cold as winter
Leaving us to pick out the splinters
One thing we can agree on is to go our separate ways
And that we will both be in a better place

I despise running in circles
let me run in squares
the stops and starts of a broken love affair
I thought we turned a corner but I stood alone as you
weren't there
I used to love winter but the cold this year has been
brutally bitter as our love began to wither
Now I cling to thoughts of spring
and hopeful of what a change in seasons will bring.

Our Snow Angels
still lay imprinted
in the week old snow
wings half-circles
of swinging giggling arms
yet they are empty now
empty like the echo
of the tv that I watch alone
of the pans that clink
with meals for one

of my footsteps walking
to an empty bedroom
echoing like my lost dreams
of what once was so real
Once I believed
we could hold vows true
but the circle was broken
Winter swept in with an icy chill
as you left
and the remembrance
of your golden band bouncing off the counter
continuously echoes
throughout the recesses of my mind.

Gazing through latticed windows
To catch the sun
Cruel April left me undone
For in the clouds of whimsy
I caught. Glittering eyes
Flimsy wispy clumsy lies
My May his charms had
Chained to December
Condemned to ponder
And Stoke sad embers
Winter's sheltered warmth in summer's brazen heat
Sometimes a chilly breeze
Is what you really need.
I won't remember how
It felt to thaw
Unwanted upon the counter
Past the expiration of our love
But toss out all notions of sell by dates
And walk away

*All alone... Embracing this
My fate.*

*Soul satiating solitude
That offers me fruit
A peace in contemplative roots.*

I feel tension pervading the space between us
like the fog rolling in...
an overwhelming plague of darkness.
Misty eyes begin flowing like rapids,
crashing upon the shores of my heart.
I'm suddenly capsized by emotions,
carried away in the current of my own thoughts.
I fear the worst about how this will play out,
but what choice do I have?
For when you truly love someone,
there are no ropes binding them to your vessel,
no anchors to hold them in place,
and no compass to direct their path.
There is only hope that when you're lost at sea,
they are the lighthouse guiding you back home.

*Storms rage incessantly roiling the dark seas
currents constantly tug and entice
lightning illuminates the hailstones of life's travails
rain and hail pelt upon my soul every waking hour
yet I remain strong and steadfast
for my anchor holds me secure in port
no chain or rope binds me
for I am free and I remain bound only by love
mesmerized by the beacon
in your eyes*

a remembrance
that always
guides me home.

Something slipped through my fingers
I lost it somewhere
I just can't recall the place

Something that was mine alone
Gone without a trace
I think it was my courage

Something doused my inner fire
left it cold and damp
please find your torch and light it

Tammy S. Thomas, *Veronica Thornton*, D.B. Hall, *Amrita Valan*, Dena Daigle, *D.B. Hall*, Brenda-Lee Ranta

Wings

Whooshing and whirring,
It's the clouds dripping onto my feathers,
Seeping into my soul
Warning its hypnotized bliss;
Waxing into creases of a new dawn.
And no more do I need feathers
Or a crown of flowers;
Only my wings suffice.
You frolic like a child,
At the notion of infusing iridescence
Into my bones,
When all I ask for is the candescence
Of embers
Yet, it took not a blink for you
To brim ebony into my hollow bones.

You take flight
A glowing bird of the night
engulfed by
magnificent wings
Soul souring
Drowning is the sky in majestic hues of sapphire
Wings dropping feathers as you dance through the hours
Whooshing and whirring
You
Take flight

Sharada Sivaraman, *Kelly Klein*

Tuesday's Gone

Meet me at the crossing
Of borrowed time,
I'll tell you about freedom,
About illusion,
The bane of life...
A life where
Stereotypes run rampant
Your skin makes you a target
Religion purges the evident...
If a heart were bullets,
My arsenal would set you free
But you see,
They've been planting seeds
Of self destruction
We convince ourselves we need a light on
That the dark is a no fly zone
That the monsters don't look like you and I...
That we're unique
If love's inside us
But when we wake up
Tuesday's gone,
Another line we've drawn
When we let time run the clock.

Time is always borrowed
But I'll meet you anywhere you choose
The crossing is the perfect place
For us to slip our comic blues
Illusion is delusional
When it's freedom that we seek
It blinds us from reality
Makes us soft and weak
We get up every morning

Put on our new expensive clothes
Hiding insecurity
Tormented by the life we chose
Those monsters sure are real to us
They are companions of the night
But it rarely makes a difference
They're around even when there's light
And love binds us a sisters
We'll cross before the morning dawn
Dance along the Milky Way
Because tomorrow Tuesday's gone

Blackened, cracked fingernails
scratch lines into the gritty earth
blood-shot eyes stare at the clock… tick-tock
does doomsday approach as Tuesday disappears
or just another day of self-destruction
in this hell we call paradise?

Monsters walk in the light
children cower in the dark
delusional billionaires piss away money
in their illusion of freedom and security
while starving people count their ribs
Religions are a mantle for sainthood
or a get out of jail free card
for the monster that makes the children cower
both of them live on borrowed time.

A schoolkid rushes by
with his bookbag on his back
and Harry Potter's latest book in his hand
oblivious to the ticking

or the monsters around him
just loving the fantasies in his head
and racing the clock to get to school.

Styx or Jordan
or just a cosmic space
the clock ticks for every soul
your time marches closer
yet none can claw closer
it cannot be stopped
love slips away in our rush
till our blood-shot eyes watch that final
tick-tock.

*I sit and stare
no solace for a wounded heart,
Tuesday morning is gone
Veined hands caress
the cup,
painted nails tap
in rhythm to her tale,
another time
another land,
a young girl
strolls village paths,
jumps from the train
tumbles carelessly in the air
I traveled with her there
on Tuesday Morning .
An ocean of dreams,
sisters with young certainty,
begin again
a curious land,*

she danced into the arms of love,
her story/my story
a family legacy,
where we came from
and who we are meant to be,
I listened and learned on Tuesday morning
Painted hands stilled,
her voice faded into memory
Tuesday mornings gone,
stories are all told
but she lives on in me

Sarah Lamar King, *Lyne Beringer*, D.B. Hall, *Tamsen Grace*

Comradery

Please give me a break
or maybe two or three.
Think a bit before you start
to spew hostility.
We all have our thoughts
on what is going on.
Let's all play with grace and love
and try to get along.
Can't we stick together
and lift our neighbors high?
Show our comradery,
let loving be our light?

It's crazy just how simple the walk is to love,
It shouldn't even matter when push comes to shove.

The deepest part of joy is learning to let go,
The heart belongs to God and only will He know.

We should strive to help each other to the very end,
Because when we share true love, we find a loyal friend.

Let us try to walk each mile loving those who need,
Embracing anyone just plants more loving seeds.

Today, be sure to love a neighbor, stranger or a friend,
And plant the gift of love to the very end.

Angela Bertoli, *Shirley Cooper*

Chain

Left with nothing but the air I breathe,
As war took it all from me…

*Destruction of my self-esteem
Ripped apart on its seam
Scars tattoo my broken heart
A battle lost right from the start*

I will not mourn
The pieces of my broken heart
Nor the loss of my last breath

*Arising from broken pieces of myself
Learning to love my roadmap of scars
I inhaled their war and breathed peace*

Peace emanated from my scarred soul
From nothingness I was made whole

*From that feeling of completeness I ran wild
A wolf set loose to feast on the delicacies life had to offer*

Generating revenue by putting bodies on the line war
brings dollars outweighing peace every time.

*When shadows fall on the ground, we face
The swords driven through our love.*

…but it was there on my knees that I gathered my strength.
I knew that redemption would soon be mine

War breaks a body and mind

But God sings into my wounds and breathes wholeness into my lifeline

It has left me bereft and on my knees, no one to turn to as they were all taken from me...

*Every battle attempting to suffocate me
but here I still stand...breathing...
alive!*

There are no tears left to cry as children stare, wide eyed, waiting for solace that never comes

*We cannot be sandwiched between two wrongs
Or pigeon hole to fit one damaging bad ideology*

I thought why life is so unfair
as I marched to take back my life again

*They fanned the fire with our flaming flag,
then fanned the flame with our burning bush,
burning bridges in between.*

I sheathe my battered soul and begin to survey the wreckage.

*Tears of brave souls rained down from the heavens,
washing away my hate and soaking me with peace.*

within dark dwellings I have witnessed the roots of evil: soul scorched by war the thirst for truth and good remains resolute. Peace is my hope.

*I struggle to stay imprisoned,
longing for parole*

The snow that falls flows with sadness,
The rain filled with anger is out of tears,
For I am a lonely traveler with no meaning…
And I will be forever forlorn and alone.

*Lost to another dose
Heroin my drug of choice
Doth on East 6th and Crocker*

We staggered forward with our bayonets; our enemy lurched towards us. We met in the same mud and fused together our hatred and our love. Years later grass and trees cover the field. But who will remember us and our expended passion?

*I will save myself
I choke.
Eyes burning,
I still fight with courage and hope.*

Do I suffocate?
Or do I extricate
Myself
My mind
My psyche
My soul
My inner being?

*I'll breathe air in you if that's what you need
to fight this war*

that lies beneath your skin.

alas but war didn't win
I still keep hope within

Sarah Lamar King, *Markus Fleiscmann,* Maggie Mae, *D.B. Hall,* Kent Rucker, *Lyne Beringer,* Veronica Thornton, *Gavin King,* Dena Daigle, *Jaz,* Donna McCabe, *Donna Sanders,* Susan E. Birch, *Mark Andrew Heathcot*e, Krishna DV, *Justin R. Hart,* Alfa, *Kelly Klein,* Aly O'Neill, *Matt Eayre,* Leah Marie Rogers, *Gocni Shindler,* Richard Milne, *Tiffany Simone,* Xavier Smith, *Sagar Singh,* Shelley Buttenhoff Miller

Here

We may no longer be a lips length apart.

Life may have seen fit
to distance our bodies
but the music has forever stitched our hearts as one.
When the night is still
and there is no more chaos for your ears to hear,
my memory will whisper a lyrical lullaby.

Have you forgotten,
it is I who resides in the stars?
My celestial silhouette will blanket your mind.
I will keep watch over you
as a song of old drifts you into dreams.

And as you rest

within your beautiful slumber
I will step...
ever so slightly upon your dreams
dancing across burgeoning clouds
With the gentle feet of angels
Blowing butterfly kisses
to the wind of your sweet silhouette
of whispering lullabies
Evoking a wave
of joyous smiles
across your cosmic seas.

Amy Noble, *Prince A. McNally*

Poverty it was You ~ The cry of the poor

Poverty it was you that turned away the heart
of the love I thought was mine,
You were unfair to me.

Poverty it was you
that made me delay going to school
when my mates got their admission,
You were unfair to me.

Poverty it was you
that made my family and friends suffer in pains
and I couldn't be of help,
You were unfair to me.

Poverty it was you
that made me hide my face
when others talked about money,
You were unfair to me.

Poverty it was you
that made me afraid of tomorrow
every time I thought about life,
You were unfair to me.

Poverty it was you
I finally rejected his friendship
because you were never there for me,
You were unfair to me.

Poverty it was you
That liquidated all my assets
Pawned my belongings to pay off debts
You were unfair to me.

Poverty it was you
That forfeited my mortgage
Took my home, left me destitute
You were unfair to me.

Poverty it was you
Who issued my divorces papers?
Split up my entire family unit
You were unfair to me.

Poverty it was you
Who signed my death warrant?
Said I hadn't paid enough health insurance
You were unfair to me.

Poverty it was you
Poverty it was you
It was you, it was you -- it was you
You were so unfair to me.

John Jave Akhimien, *Mark Andrew Heathcote*

Fire of the Phoenix

She's fire, burning eternally unbidden
She's fueled by the sun and the gift of its brilliance
Her Phoenix soul burns from ashes to flame
Mountain tops beckon her as she takes flight time and again
She's too hot to the touch, but her burn is like being kissed
by the very rays that feed her bones
She's untamable, when she lands on your door it will be of
her own accord
Her magic is words, verses, and tales, they will awaken the
ways to a new world
A fiery goddess with a gift from the starts
I am that fire, I am the Phoenix that burns through the night

He is the howl from wolves of the past
He runs through time's fields and dances on moonbeams
His spirit shifts from light to mist
Forests call his name as he walks silently through history
He is fierce to behold, but his touch bestows healing and
rejuvenated hope
He is untamable, if he comes to you it is only for a moment
His magic is pain, heartache and sorrow, destroyed and
recreated as hope and love
An ancient spirit of timeless youth
I am the smile in the dark, the call of the wilderness

Jesica Nodarse, *Matt Eayre*

Hope

Hope,
such a simple word
for the motivating force of life.
this tired heart
has carried burnt-out torches
for endless miles,
searching for a spark.

*...and when your hope begins to wane,
as quickly as your flame flickers
and fades
I will harness the fiery coals
that branded your heart.
And I will use them
to transform the pain and darkness
into hollowed ground
that is illuminated by my love.*

and on my knees
warm and safe
I will worship your heart
with every breath

Matt Eayre, *Alfa*, Matt Eayre

Doubt

Bewildered by the sight of you
Your mannerisms
So odd and abstruse
From the way you breathe
To the food you eat
You're incomprehensible
To every fiber of me

A sentry leopard on high
Black & white
Basking in the midday sun
Wonders why chameleons
Change colour in response
To all other passing scenes
Is it to find merit without risk
Why qualm about appearances
About politics look at me,
I've got, Charm & Charisma
With all your different guises
I doubt even you
Can spot the difference.

Yet here I am, at your door
Midnight calling
The one I adore

When the Sun Returns to the sky,
After the storm has passed by,
Will you see the world through different eyes,
Know that you survived and your alive,
When you challenge the clouds of doubt
Know they don't know what they are on about,
When you take on the world again,

Live the life of your dreams,
When the Sun returns to the sky,
There are still questions you don't know why,
When the clouds of grey have faded away,
Picture that waterfall once again,
The twinkle is there, the spark you want to share,
The dreams and schemes that is so real,
Looking at life through different eyes,
When the sun returns to the sky.

Night has ended
the dark veil gone
Light shines as you open your eyes
A new day, new thoughts
Will you create a new you?
Will you see through different eyes
The problems no longer insurmountable
A glint, a spark of hope
When the sun returns to the sky

Xavier Smith, *Mark Andrew Heathcote*, Maggie Mae, *Steve Lay*, Amanda J. Evans

Concrete Jungle

A pride hunts in the concrete jungle
long-limbed gazelles narrowly escape
darting into protected havens
marked by pulsating lights
and rhythmic beats.

Hot steamy nights lulling the prey
making connections for another day
Like jackals they circle endlessly
grinning like corpses
as they make their play.

Nearby hear the roaring hippos
as they bathe in opulent luxury
amid champagne waters
of wall street's oasis
sharing with trumpeting elephants
but keeping all others at bay.

The flash of greenbacks mesmerizes
dangle that carrot before their eyes
see the yearning and glassy-eyed stare
invade their soul, strip them bare
buy them and sell them
what do you care?

Predators and players
lurk behind every blade of grass
footprints everywhere
read the signs on your trail.

Fakers and takers,
movers and shakers

with crocodile grins
He who dares wins
Choose your side
herd or pride

Who are you
and who will you be
standing at life's dusky door?

D.B. Hall, Susan E. Birch

Broken Lands

Awash with hurt
Pride ground into dirt
Hoodie up, head down
Blinders on, perma-frown
Infused with pain
Driven to insanity's plane
Earbuds in, iPod on blast
Blasting away the past
Under a veil of blindness
Wandering in darkness

Anonymity
Is now the new me
Lost in life twists
Scars on wrists,
Scars on my soul
Condemned to never be whole
Fuck me,
FUCK me
And fuck you too
Now others wander lost here
Souls scream in angst, no-one hears
Alone in the broken lands
Created by abusive hands
Souls scream
But no one hears
As they avoid
Abusive hands

The sun shines bland indifferent
The roads and shrubberies brilliant
The ground hard as diamond under feet
I'm a poet who has lost his beat.

In these lands they break and tame you down
Hand you blinkers so hide behind it
Cover your frown
Suppress your screams no one will help
Smile your vacancy, else look down.

Feelings die in the air, they heat up
Rise and vaporize
The cold angels of death shall gather us,
Reap our lycra lives,
Promised Lego Land of lies
Where men are trained like mice
To lose their souls in the seductive maze
The purpose of life
Shouldn't ever have been
This dumb rat race.

Kent Rucker, *Amrita Valan*

Unspoken

Words are wonderful
When spoken from heart
Bringing out from inside
Those unspoken thoughts

How lucky are those ears
That get to hear
Those wonderful words
Spoken from the heart of the heart

How lucky is that eye
That gets to see
Those unspoken words
Spoken from the eyes with a heart

How intriguing is that eye
That speaks to me
In the language of gazes
Some long, some short

Listening in silence
I hear the noise
Of unspoken word
and untold thoughts

Let me enjoy
Sitting in silence
The noise of silence
Evoking a stream of thoughts!

Many times
Have words cut deep
Wounding my heart

Slicing my self-esteem
Often words have been
Murderous
Spoken with ignorance
Words describe
What is in need
What is seen
They are reasons for tears
Explanation of fears
Words ignite like fire
Spin webs of liars
Spoken soft with desire
Spoken in trust
Buried with dust
Words can heal
But also steal
They can be warm
Cold or strong
A word spoken
A word written
No matter the creed
It is not forbidden
Words can be enlightening
Words can be inspiring
Fighting and biting
Productive or destructive
My favorite are hers
Very seductive
Progressive not obsessive
Even in silence a word is heard
In a kiss from a heart
Unspoken in her eyes
Read in verse and rhymes

On her lips
Even by blind fingertips

Krishna DV, *Markus Fleischmann*

Our Time

This was our time
the glory of our youth
etching memories
we would later cherish
as we toiled in the days
of our regrets.

*So many regrets linger
until it is stale upon the air
it lingers in the cigarette smoke
curling over a stack of bills upon the table
they stare back at him
from a variety of refrigerator pictures
sent from blue-eyed kids
he barely ever gets to see
they reflect deep from within a tortured soul
every morning as he shaves
and when the early morn sun
kisses a faded handmade sun charm
that sits over the kitchen sink
he takes his last drink of coffee
and rinses his cup
flicks the charm shining in the sun
remembering the glorious days of his youth
and the sunshiny days after
the time of his glory
and leaves to face another grueling day
driving down streets with no character
names he can't remember
in a place he still can't call home.*

If I live as they expect then I'm living as if I'm their
personal pet leaving me nothing except what they expect.

ELEVEN YEARS OLD.......
Please, is there someone out there
who speaks my language?
Will you talk to me soulfully
Like Keats does?
Will you make your words mellifluous
so they flow through my soul
as Yeats does?
Can you speak in Shakespearean vein?
Write a sonnet to tell me I am sane
and not some alien shame
planted in the wrong place
at the wrong time.
I am waiting quietly in the silent night
for someone to understand my plight.
I am trapped in a world I don't understand.
Someone speak to me please!
I am lost in a foreign land.

I live for the moment
Regrets nothing and sorry I am not
For who I am and what I maybe
Is still a mystery
I won't dwell on what ifs
And how it could be
All I know is that I could only be me

The sandcastles have crumbled
with the weight of years
and those once bright seashells
are tarnished and worn.

Life makes fools of us all eventually

And we live on innocent memories
that become artefacts discarded
that are returned from the ashes
the fire that burns reignited
must be controlled to burn
steadily brighter
and unite us all in the appreciation
of what we have and share
in common goals and understanding
so we can build
and inherit a much better future

Kent Rucker, *D.B.Hall*, Veronica Thornton, *Susan E. Birch*, Tammy S. Thomas, *Susan E. Birch*, Mark Andrew Heathcote

A Beginner's Fortune

Trembling
I can't seem to shake free the words
For this den of literary nobles
Who blaze ever-bright

*Stars shine bright
as they dance with Webster
he fills their inkwells
will magical words
every time I get close
someone swirls him away
at the end of the night
I am alone in the den
with my empty inkwell
and a dry pen
Woe is me
a terrible dancer
and hapless poet.*

William Wright Jr., *D.B. Hall*

Steps

The forge is vehement as we hone our daggers whole; hell fire scourge as we groan the toils of propaganda. Frost recounts the streetlamp flicker as total war seems so distant from a television screen. It ices soul a'plenty a frigid heart, removed twice over from humankind. Recount the steps towards perceived sanity and realize all that you've done wrong. Dante, you saint, descend us to the pit in which we came. For we are undeserving of our god and life abound!
Senses These fragile times challenges
snuffed to scythe the root of all evil. Amen.

Each one of us to dig deeper into
our very essence whilst making sense
of a darkening halo -
Nation against nation man against
woman child against parent
citizen against government
student against teacher
believer against religion
a new war threatening this human mission -
We question argue resist
insist confess regress escape
lie hide confide even willing
to alter our identity in this
oddity we call life -
It's time to reorganize
this human hive...

Josh Dale, *Don Beukes*

Day of Remembrance

A full life wheels in reverse
In these few and solemn hours
Brimming,
With old friends and foes

> *Where history died*
> *To repeat once more*
> *No lesson learned*
> *No flag unfurled*
> *Lay down their arms*
> *That lost their legs*
> *No lesson learned*
> *From the mouth of the dead*

The whirling wheel
Twirls and reels
The only emotion
Is an unholy notion;
A curse.
It spun a cocoon
Breeds a butterfly.
It share pleasure
With consequences of eternal pressure.
A day never to forget
For in satisfaction of life
We deprive the soul of his

> *Reliving all the memories,*
> *the joys and the woes,*
> *bumping into past people,*
> *the good and the bad,*
> *cleansing the soul,*
> *so peace can be had*

William Wright Jr., *Brenda-Lee Ranta*, Dagu Shangevlumun, *Donna McCabe*

Reality's Sorrow

My reality is sorrow… a cold hard pillow
Bearing regret's thin torn blanket
Haunting me… A truth I can't swallow
A harsh cemetery of lies I can't forget

> *Preyed upon by my dreams*
> *And nightmares when I wake,*
> *No escape*
> *Hide the key to indecision,*
> *Take a breath or join them,*
> *When everything I love*
> *Falls like rain…*

> Into my pit of despair
> When will I wake
> When will I sleep
> My reality is sorrow…

> *Darkness draped my soul*
> *after our moons were shattered*
> *and light was ripped from the night*
> *the rain of regret was icy pain*
> *upon my blanket of sorrow*
> *I swallowed my hope*
> *this pit untouched by light*
> *becomes my grave*

Kent Rucker, *Sarah Lamar King*, Maggie Mae, *D.B. Hall*

Meant to Be

If only this fragile little heart
knew the language of lust.
But it's nothing but a sentimental fool,
Craving for arms to hold it,
Dreaming about eyes it can wake up to,
Broken too many times,
Taped, bandaged and ready to love again,
Writing poetries in a world full of dyslexics
Taking pictures, for a crowd that's blind,
Why can't it be flooded with lust,
Why can't it just let it be,
Why can't it just accept,
For some, forever's are not meant to be.

If only this lustful hunger
knew how to be vulnerable.
never anything but a moment of pleasure,
longing for a quiet conversation
hoping for a connection not based on animal need,
given in to temptation,
too many times
cleaned, refreshed and waiting to be used again,
reading philosophy in a world full of instant gratification,
posing for cameras while searching for depth
why can't it be rising to the heavens
why can't it be anything but lonely,
why can't it be understood,
for some, a touch is not enough.

Sagar Singh, *Matt Eayre*

Crevices of Pain

I hid my pain
Deep within the crevice
Of my jagged heart
Deep down in its shadowy reaches
Void of fluttering emotions
Barren of fruitless hope
I keep it where my soul
Is still wrapped in
The barbed wire web of lies
I allowed you to spin
Hidden amongst the scriptures
Of a forgotten time
Still engraved deep into its
Fleshly cold walls
Thine love
Cold steel against my heart
Has thou cast into my soul
Trickling is my hope
In thine eternity still
For nor does the sun
Shine bright at twilight
As the moon dies at midnight
Longing has thou left me blind
Questing for my heart's sight
A flower reaching for rain
I wilt inside from mine pain

I am a dandelion among the dead roses
Decaying petals and tears
Soak into the crevices of my heart
And are the sustenance
For my flower of hope
Reaching upwards

For the sunshine
Of your love
Alas, tis but a memory
In the twilight o my days
A self-inflicted penance
For I worshipped the scriptures of your truths
And believed the aberrations of your lies
The writings on the wall
Led me
To the garden of real truth
My world erupted in reality
The veil was lifted from my eyes
I could see clearly
Chaos and catastrophe ensued
And love died at midnight
Yet in the twilight of my days
I am dandelion among the decay
Reaching past the veil for my sunshine.

Broken syllables bleed
In fragmented phrases,
Weeping all night.
I try to gather them
Like an angler
Caught in a turbulent sea.
I fuse the phrases,
Dig the metaphors
Out of empty words,
Squeeze their emotions,
Pepper them with figures,
And poetry is born.

Markus Fleischmann, *Kent Rucker*, Debasish Mishra

An Anthology of Collaborations

Writers Block

Searching my mind
For words to say
Echoes of nothingness
Meet my attention
Silence
Empty crevices
No voice to speak, cry out, verbalize my pain
Trapped in this frozen reverie
I seek solace that will never be mine
Ice sculptures encase
My freedom speech
I wait in solitude
Frozen in time
Flickers and whispers
Brush past, never sticking
I wait
Longing for the thaw
The heat of words
My fire breathing dragon
I wait
Pen in hand
Senses sharp
Whispers close
I feel the burn
My frozen reverie
Softens with a single word
Then sentence by sentence
The furnace ignites
My dragon roars once more

A muse's tiny spark grow into a roaring fire?
Creates within us an insatiable itching desire?
Stories itch their way throughout your brain?

Multiples ideas flowing on multiple planes

We can feel the coming tumbling flow
We need to get away, we have got to go
Where can we go to escape so we can write?
Our struggle is real, this is our poetic plight

I for one, will never be famous in history
Few will ever remember my words or me
Yes, I realize that, yet I continue to scribble
My blessing and my curse this poetic dribble

Many poets around the world share my zeal
They understand this burn, the yearn is real
Solitary orbs light houses all hours of the night
As passionate poets labor over their write

Poetry should never be ONLY read and heard
It is not just casual written and spoken word
No, their open hearts penned should be felt
Like caresses on the neck or lashes with a belt

Our poet's eyes have cried over poems that died
The writes that you read are ones that survived
Lines march across papers crinkled with their tears
Containing all their hopes, dreams and even fears

Yet all of a poet's work is not available to be read
In their darkest places, you are not allowed to tread
That is their holy grail, where only they can play
Perchance in death, you can hear what they say?

The sun creeps lower

Merging with the horizon
before retreating into slumber
The moon begins its nightly watch

Sleepy souls retreat to beds
A poet flirts with thoughts
In his restless head
A verse
A rhyme
A word on a line
Like dreams to the rest
His thoughts
Become familiar guest
As the moon stands watch
As stars twinkle bright
He ponders the reasons
Of what to write
Answering his nightly invite

The ice spreads quickly
under plummeting temperatures,
freezing everything in it's grasp,
it has no conscience or empathy,
as you're caught up in its grasp,
Until the sun rises once more,
bringing heat and warmth to the land,
rises ever higher in the sky
the ice will contract and expand.

The poet weeps
At dawns light
The nights muse
Fading from sight

An Anthology of Collaborations

The warmth day brings
Freezes his words
As it melts the landscape

Amanda J. Evans, *D.B. Hall*, Amanda J. Evans, *Markus Fleiscmann*, Donna McCabe, *Maggie Mae*

Memories

If you just let go,
you will be free
To love what you know
and know what you see

reach into the flame
and don't fear the heat
give hope a name
and hear it's heart beat

time, it is nothing
existence is a fable
we create what we eat
when we sit at the table

it really doesn't matter
if you're foolish or smart
as long as you live life
straight from your heart

If you let go,
love will catch you,
doves coo, soft and low
When you let go,
love is a vision,
angels sing, rivers flow

Facts in our head,
truth in our heart
Life is a thread,
love is an art

Matt Eayre, *Hugh Dysart*

Infernos

Oh darling...
you think your words are fire
and you stand there
waiting to watch me burn
but obviously
you didn't know me at all.
Embers run through my veins
and my heart has been
through many seas of flames.
There will be no piles
of ashes to rummage through.
I devour infernos in rations
to conserve my sanity

My dear
It wasn't the fire in my words
You had to defend against
It was the smoke
That held your burning scent
You may have been Phoenix born
In flames you may have made your home
You may have heated fortitude
But your flames can't ignite again
I've stolen your oxygen

Donna J. Sanders, *Markus Fleischmann*

Traveler

The moon traveled through my veins
and then my skin awakened
and crawled with wondrous anticipation

There I found the wildness
that matched my own
and his howled calls
that brought me home

> *The moon brought me peace today*
> *When I saw the reflection*
> *Of love in her wild eyes*

Raven Nicole, *Maggie Mae*

Interred Truth

'They laid truth down again,
Cribbed, cabined and confined,
Prefer to call it alternative facts,
Fake news is intertwined,
With garbage, guff and weasel words,
Sucked dry of life like sand,
They fill the mind with cotton wool,
You know longer understand,
Or want to; it's easier to bang your head,
Against a wall of brick,
It feels so good when you stop,
Perhaps that is their trick.
Yet think of the Gettysburg address,
Its words of meaning deep,
Against what passes for today,
How the fall is steep.
Yes they laid truth in its narrow grave,
The headstone chiseled drear,
'Truth lies interred below, stranger shed a tear.'

> Six feet under, in a shallow grave lies a lament.
> The tombstone in black granite, has its noble intent.
> They have buried here the Whole Truth, in deep seated fear
> If resurrection happens,
> a mausoleum may not last for years
> Marble and gilded letters, eulogized but so unfortunately
> The Dead one is not dead, he sleepwalks, you can see
> When these dark clouds rise, and blood becomes red again,
> Lies shall vanish, the soil shall nourish not the villain.
> The miasma gone, let there be light for all to see
> The meek shall rise, and Truth alone run free...

Richard Milne, *Kanchan Bhattacharya*

When I Die

I will sleep
To the lies
I gave credence.

When I die...

I will wake
To the joy
Of truth
I doubted often.

When I die...

I will be
A convict,,
To walk the maze.
A beast so vain

When I die...

I'll stand guilty
To the science of truth
Or by craft
Of lies
Be exonerated

The final truth is
our life
and our consciousness
is what we perceive
through our sensory organs
and it's interpretation in the brain.

Truth and lies are samples of life
a set of directions
created by social imposition

Death is an answer
on its on
will it open other doors
or are we going just fade from memory?

When I die...
truth may not be barred from me again

Death is an answer
on its on
will it open other doors
or are we going just fade from memory?

When I die...
truth may not be barred from me again

Dagu Shangevlumun, *Kanchan Bhattacharya*, Dagu Shangevlumun

Job of Living

It comes
Creeping in
So subtle sometimes
Suddenly struck
Like lightening
Flashes of dark thoughts
Bring sorrowing emotions
Settling in
Taking over my
Very heart and body
Lethargy
Hopelessness
Helplessness
As to what my
Next step should be
How impossible it is
To get back to the
Job of living

The harshness of life
is like ivy and moss
creeping on a stone wall
overtaking all
till stones see no light.
Darkness must be repelled
for in light I find hope
I find my salvation.
yet even without it
I survive
this job of living.

Kent Rucker, *Shelly Buttenhoff Miller*

My Enemy/My Friend

Darkness is my enemy
Yet still my closest friend
And sometimes words get tangled up
But they help my spirit mend
Writing is my legacy
A wager that I'll hedge
It keeps me off the precipice
When I teeter on the edge
And when the sun is setting
The shadows come to dance
Waltzing pass the midnight moon
With nothing left to chance

I pen my thoughts and become a sage
Taking tentative steps in rhythm
I garden with words and set the stage
Making each paragraph and line mine
And as dawns light touches the page
I am struck by what has evolved
What once was hard and cultivated
And looked forced and unresolved
Now looks effortless and organic
And where once was darkness
Now there is only a botanic-
Garden of flowering goblets.

Lyne Beringer, *Mark Andrew Heathcote*

Smoked

He blew her off
as he always did before
treated her secondhand
like another
could be pulled from the pack.

From a distance
I watched their stormy exchange
saw her phoenix awakened
and come soaring up
from the scorned ashes.

Finally aware
he desperately grasped
a double handful of empty vapors
left in her smoldering trail.

> *Vapors rise in the icy mist*
> *they would be seductive*
> *in the azure moonlight*
> *if not for the bed of ashes*
> *from which they rise.*
>
> *A bed with our passionate history*
> *consumed by my flames of ignorance*
> *and rebuilt as my lonely prison*
> *where alone I smolder*
> *shackled to your memory.*

She had been destroyed too many times to count
and she was certain that he was no different from the rest.
Although that smile of his could ignite flames
in the coldest of hearts,

she had no regard for weak emotions
such as lust…not anymore.
You see betrayal has the power to transform
even the hottest of infernos into frigid icebergs

She arises from the ashes of which he left her,
Scorned...
Her revenge is sweet
Knocking him down to his feet,
Begging her for mercy as he plead his case
She laughs and whispers... meet your fate

Empty promises
like vapour trails,
no true ending and
no real depth.
I have breathed in
your fragrant lies
for far too long.
Take another shot,
smoke another cigarette
whilst you watch me leave.
I have discovered my phoenix.
Watch me rise above.

Red as blood my wings were earned
Scorched by your constant shaming heart
Heavy the burden of duty
Carried out
Now I shrug you off for a brand-new start
Yes, I bled too when yours I was
Unaware that I had some worth
Now feel the air part as I ascend

An Anthology of Collaborations

Let my grace be legacy in your days of lent.

D.B. Hall, *Kent Rucker*, Dena Daigle, *Tammy S. Thomas*,
Susan E. Birch, *Amrita Valan*

Fly

One last kiss
to ease my hearts retreat,
Your skin wraps me in feather,
I'll take flight now that you're here,
Whisper my name in Angels' ears,
My wings will take me home,
I'll wait for you there.

It takes but a single kiss
To know heaven
Dreams fly light on feathered wings
Whispers roll on golden tongue
Playing a heart's melody
On a harp silver strung
One kiss
No more
To close forever bound
Heaven's door

Satan, well he has another abode
And he can't join you there
tempting as an antidote
A cure to all his melancholy
His no good evil despair
you couldn't pay that fare
but one more kiss
you can't resist
temptation
after, which
you will learn to desist.

Sarah Lamar King, *Markus Fleischmann,* Mark Heathcote

Ice to the Fire

I am the ice to your fire
A blanket of snow
Just outside of your glow
The ash of a funeral pyre
I am the cold to your heat
All frigid and numb
Your warmth will succumb
Like a withering vine in retreat
I am the frost to your flame
A devilish Queen
Your light has been seen
Now winter is calling your name

*I am the rhythm and the rhyme
in the songs of enchanted love birds*

*I am that fiery flame
the coldness of your heart desperately yearns to feel*

*I am that ever bright
beacon of light*

*That which compels you
to rise from the darkness of your shadowed past*

*I am that deep and persistent burning
that forever dwells in the echos of your heart*

*I am but love slowly transforming your ice sculpture
into a boiling river ... of ever-flowing passion.*

I was born of heat and fire

You are the wildfire in my fingers
Your skin is branded to these hands
Night after endless night
Our union serves as the match striking my mind.
I swirl in the sweat of a million poetic variations.
I am the pyromaniac burning hot for you
Spitting flames of memory
Igniting blank pages.
Everyone should know this heat

Lyne Beringer, *Prince A.McNally*, Amy Noble

Fevered Twilight, Lost and Fading

Fevered twilight lost and fading
serenading passing time
slow we drift through dreams to sift
and dare to dance divine
Tossed in fevered twilight
lost across the night's display
stars like tiny diamonds
in their dazzling arrays
Yet none are mine in calling
falling fast in passing night
this serenade an homage paid
where dreams esteem to die
Wait still her words are stirring
blurring time a true divine
and thoughts are now returning
burning pleasure treasured time,
Cool and calm now goes this passing
once again in dreams to play
twilight serenading to the coming of the day

You serenade me at twilight
and save me from the void
you let me hear the voice
that drifts through my dreams.
The fevered skies billow
like tussled ebony sheets
tangled in brilliant constellations
rearranging encoded messages
for those who ride
the sacred wings of love.
Time immortal is mine
a pleasure shared with you
illuminated in moments

frozen in memories
like puppets on a stage
yet perpetual reality
as we dance under the star's display.
The world can see our nothing
for our love is a private array
a serenading of the twilight
that gives the diamonds their shine
in the sanctuary of our day.

Aaron Johnson, *Kent Rucker*

Night's Battle

And the nights are strung together by days,
both seeking principality....
both willing pawns in a war
that rages between the sun and the moon

*Just as my heart and my mind
Life quarrels death, steady unrest
Challenging each one's course
Drowning in regrets,
Concede with wings into the night
My companion, swallow me whole
But once again enticed
The suns predictable rise
As day devours night,
Dawn sweeps me away,
Strung together by hope.*

Lyne Beringer, *Sarah Lamar King*

Fight

Each step in this life a struggle
fighting to hold it all up
to hold it all in
hold it together... this my life

Fighting scratching clawing
all day ... everyday

To the point of surrender
till words of wisdom
from beyond the veil
unchained my fettered mind
freed me of my worrisome weights
I know not why I burdened myself for so long.

Abandoning my shackles at the foot of the veil
stepping light footed away
on the wings of encouragement's whispers
garner our strength where we can.

> *Heavy laden footsteps weighing
> down my brittle soul
> Strugglin' to keep the pieces
> together, to hold on to what
> makes me strong -*
>
> *Each amber breath elongated
> chest heaving daily mourning
> emotions churning my spiritual
> yearning.*
>
> *My essence riddled with
> fatigue yet a soothing*

whisper heals my murky
interior - Calming my pulsating
fear, each beat another
burden liberated

Chains melting
our collective voices
shouting lamenting
seeking questioning
answering -

Just breathe...

Sometimes the dark feels
heavy and menacing
as if light has forgotten your name
the road, narrow and absent
of gentle reprieves
is cast before you
there are no hands to hold
or warm voices
to slice through the cold
the tempest is yours alone
you did not ask for it and yet it answers
there was no kneeling on your part
and yet it surrounds you like a prayer
through covered ears
you hear its voice perfectly
it is the antagonist
to all which aspires
to wrap you in light
but...there you are
mind fragmented, body sore

An Anthology of Collaborations

and clothes tattered, the course is yours
so it must be stayed, for there is a light
peeking from the clouds
which can only be shone
piecemeal through the cracks
in your armor

D.B.Hall, *Don Beukes*, Jeffery Martin

Frigid

The world has gone frigid, my lover.
The gnawing wind has bit our guardian moon,
broken in its crescent cover.
I feel as if I've lost the protection
of Lady Liberty's compassionate promise...
I have gone frigid, my lover.
The cold current blusters on my brittle limbs,
hiding within its hidden howling hymns.
I feel like I am skating on thin ice,
afraid to stand on my perilous point...
The world has gone frigid, my lover.
I feel frozen by this bitter moment in time,
awaiting our resurgent heat to melt it all away,
before our frostbitten limbs have nothing to stand on,
while we still can thaw the cold front of today...
The world has gone frigid, my lover.
I hope I haven't gone rigid...

The gnawing wind is sanctioned
By the queen of frozen things
The moon is her companion
Frigid is her gift...the one she always brings
Lady Liberty fell away
Through brittle sheets of ice
Money and all that power
Crushing promised paradise
Rigid is a state of mind
It feeds on every thought
Making you a prisoner
Long before you know you're caught
And the cold keeps getting colder
Time never was a friend
Numb is now in fashion

A gift from the gnawing wind

Justin R. Hart, *Lyne Beringer*

Freedom

Ripped apart
by guilt and shame
I was scorched
in the flames
My freedom
Is in your name.

Savage fires burn untamed
Fueling my feverish shame
Ember scorched
My heart now bears
Charcoal blackened fears
A hell's inferno
Quenched by the drops
Of my uninvited tears
As I find release
Of shackles and chain
Freedom found in your name

D.B. Hall, *Markus Fleischmann*

Can't Escape

You erased your tracks
As you left,
Hoping the past couldn't find you,
Still, you wake up with regret,
Questioning demons asleep inside you...
And I forgive you
As I forget you
Distortion suits your face now.
The love that you adorned
Becomes your crown of thorns now.
Masks aside, upon the mirror,
It's not my ghost you see,
You've haunted yourself for years,
Nothing left for me...

So run away
And flee
It's your face, your being
I no longer want to see

My hidden desolation
My visible desperation
Will eventually subside
But from now until death
With me, it will reside
Can't escape

My soul is empty
Of the promises instilled
with me unfulfilled
Love turns to hate
Hoping you meet your fate
I regret the day we met

The memories will not let me forget
Fade out into darkness to...
Escape

Sarah Lamar King, *Xavier Smith*, Tammy S. Thomas

Broken Approbation

Awake
In the early morning
Because I'm still in the mourning
Phase
Fade away
Fade away
It absconds with my soul
It leaves me with this hole
And I say to him
And I say to her
And I say to them
"Can you fill it?"
"Can you feel it?"

Fade away.... Fade away
C'mon around
On the next darkest day
If you steal it
Then you'll feel it
It's just shadows out to play....

Xavier Smith, *Lyne Beringer*

Walk With Me

Walk with me
Over and over again
Stroll these...empty
Cobblestone streets

*Day after day
hobnailed shoes echo
over empty
cobblestone streets
my hand reaches for yours
always a veil away
pass on through
walk with me
don't let my heart echo
alone.*

Walk with me
On starlight roads
Let your skin be kissed by
Winds of hope
Dream with me
On pillows of clouds
Silence your fears
Pleadingly shout
Let go of your guest
Sorrow and doubt
Take my hand
Walk about
Feel the grass
Part beneath your feet
Begging you to return this way
Hello, does the tree
In wind sway

An Anthology of Collaborations

As we journey on our way
To starlit sands and calming seas
Azure sky and blissful dreams
Walk with me
On world's edge
Feel release of daily stress
Find yourself on this road
A life so long and broad
I'll show you where
You truly belong
Like a misplaced note
In a melodic song
Of you the Angel's sing along
Fiery daybreak
Purple Dawn
Take my hand
Walk along

Gocni Schindler, *Kent Rucker*, Markus Fleischmann

An Anthology of Collaborations

Moments

Living in moments,
waves of grey...The frigid womb
Of yesterday

For what once contrived
Dies within its frozen lies
Grace, shall bring her home

Hold near
The things that you love,

Spring will bloom a woman—
Summer
Will leave you,

Painted leaves
Hungry in Orange
And the lonely fires of Winter's Corazon
Will be all that's left

To turn you...

Sarah Lamar King, *Brenda-Lee Ranta*, Wjweigand

An Anthology of Collaborations

Creative Talents Unleashed

Creative Talents Unleashed is an independent publishing group that offers writers an opportunity to share their writing talents with the world. We are committed to fostering and honoring the work of writers of all cultures. Our publishing group offers writing tips to assist writers in continued growth and learning, daily writing prompts and challenges to keep the writers mind sharp, marketing and events, as well as a variety of yearly publishing opportunities. We are honored to be assisting writers in the journey of becoming published authors.

www.ctupublishinggroup.com

For More Information Contact:

Creativetalentsunleashed@aol.com

Website: www.ctupublishinggroup.com

Blog: www.creativetalentunleashed.com

www.ingramcontent.com/pod-product-compliance
Lightning Source LLC
Chambersburg PA
CBHW071306040426
42444CB00009B/1899